YOUR KNOWLEDGE HAS VALUE

Bibliographic information published by the German National Library:

The German National Library lists this publication in the National Bibliography; detailed bibliographic data are available on the Internet at http://dnb.dnb.de .

Imprint:

Copyright © 2016 GRIN Verlag, Open Publishing GmbH
Print and binding: Books on Demand GmbH, Norderstedt Germany
ISBN: 9783668225121

This book at GRIN:

http://www.grin.com/en/e-book/323612/mergers-and-acquisitions-types-and-moti-vations-for-a-deal

Kristina Kraft

Mergers and Acquisitions. Types and Motivations for a Deal

GRIN Publishing

GRIN - Your knowledge has value

Since its foundation in 1998, GRIN has specialized in publishing academic texts by students, college teachers and other academics as e-book and printed book. The website www.grin.com is an ideal platform for presenting term papers, final papers, scientific essays, dissertations and specialist books.

Visit us on the internet:

http://www.grin.com/

http://www.facebook.com/grincom

http://www.twitter.com/grin_com

This paper was written by an author whose mother tongue is not English. Please excuse any mistakes or inconsistencies.

List of tables

Inhalt

1. Introduction

With the diagram seeing below we want to show you, that only within seven years there are in average 74.000 transactions per year all over the world. Mergers and acquisitions take place since decades and will continue. There is a lot of facts about benefits, about the risks or new methods to be profitable in a merger or an acquisition. A lot of literature show us that more than about 60% [1]of the mergers and acquisitions providing to be a failure. Besides of the high failure rates we want to show in this project paper deal motivations for mergers and acquisitions.

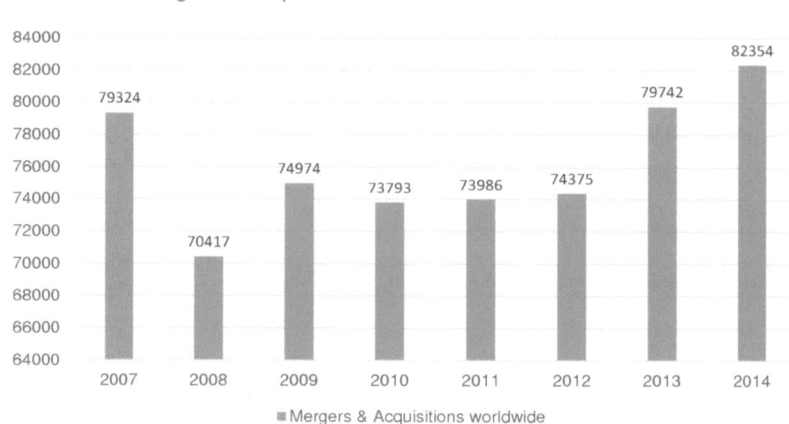

Mergers & Acquisitions worldwide 2007 - 2014

Graph 1 - Statista: http://de.statista.com/statistik/daten/studie/399031/umfrage/anzahl-der-weltweiten-munda-deals/

2. Difference between Mergers and Acquisitions

We often read the expression "Mergers and Acquisitions" in the same connection or the expressions are switched. However, we have to note that these are different meanings. In general we can say that "Mergers and Acquisitions" happens when two or more companies unite. Either completely or only partially. This process is a long-term process.

When we talk about merger it means that two or more companies combining and become a new company, when we talk about acquisition it means that one company buys another and there is not created a new company.

---

[1] Marcus Wimmer, M&A course, winter term 2015

The main differences between mergers and acquisitions are:

- Size
- Ownership
- Management control[2]

2.1 Merger

A merger is a fusion between two or more legally and economically independent enterprises. The "giving up of an enterprise" is characterized by the fact that an enterprise transfers its property on the partner and is integrated into this. What also means it loses its previous legal and economic independence at the same time.

However, at a classic merger a new company is created by the partners so that after the transmission of assets they are equal owners of this new created company.

This is a form of the merger often chosen to the public at which the contributions of the merging partner enterprises shall correspond to a 1:1 relationship in the ideal case. It has to be noticed that in most cases in the practice shows that when it comes to the compilation of the management positions that equal rights can hardly be found. It seems obviously important that at least in public for no partner the image of the "taken" initiates.[3]

2.1.1 Different types of mergers

2.1.1.1 Vertical Mergers

In a vertical merger a company buys suppliers or customers which are often involved into the production or sales process. Both are producing the same product or services, but the only difference is the level of the production. Most often the logic behind merger is to restrict supply to competitors, to create a greater market share, revenues and profits. Vertical mergers also offer cost saving and a higher margin of profit. Also they can increase synergies created by merging firms that would be more efficient operating as one.

Example

Clothing Store XY takes over a textile factory. The stage of factory is different but it's the same industry. These kinds of merger are usually undertaken to avoid interruption in supply and to secure supply of essential goods.

---

[2] Brain Coyle: Mergers and Acquisitions, p. 2
[3] Brain Coyle: Mergers and Acquisitions, p. 2

2.1.1.2 Horizontal Mergers

A horizontal merger happen when a company merges or takes over a competitor, a company which is in the same industry and at the same stage of production. The benefit is that it encourage cost efficiency, eliminates competition, and creates a new, larger organization with more market share, profits and earnings. Moreover, it also offers economies of scale due to increase in size as average cost decline due to higher production volume. These kinds of merger also encourage cost efficiency.

Example

A horizontal merge between Daimler and Chrysler this companies operations had been very similar as the both are producing middle-class and high-class cars.[4]

2.1.1.3 Product Extension

Is a situation where merger takes place between two businesses dealing with products which relate to each other. Buy complementary goods allows the merging companies to fill their portfolio and get access to bigger set of consumers. As a result, they earn higher profits.

Example

An Example of this is the acquisition of Mobilink Telecom Inc. by Broadcom. Broadcom deals in the manufacturing Bluetooth personal area network hardware systems while the other one deals in the manufacturing of product designs for handsets that are provided with the Global System for Mobile Communications technology. It is estimate that the products of Broadcom would be complementing the wireless products of Mobilink Telecom Inc.[5]

2.1.1.4 Market Extension

A market extension merger is similar to horizontal mergers; it takes place between two companies dealing with same products. The difference is that they are not in direct competition because they compete in different markets. By merging, companies can get access to a bigger client base and a bigger market.

Example

Eagle Bancshares holds one of the ten biggest banks in the metropolitan Atlanta region as far as deposit market share is concerned. One of the major benefits of the acquisition between Eagle Bancshares and RBC is that this acquisition enables the RBC to go ahead

---

[4] N.N., www.mbda.gov, 2015
[5] N.N, www.mbda.gov, 2015

with its growth operations in the North American market. With the help of this acquisition RBC has got a chance to deal in the financial market of Atlanta, which is among the leading upcoming financial markets in the USA. This move would allow RBC to diversify its base of operations.[6]

2.1.1.5 Conglomerate

It is an unrelated type of mergers it means the mergers are in different market businesses. This kind of merger is typically part of a desire on the part of one company to grow its financial wealth. By merging with a completely unrelated gains a revenue stream in many types of industries. Another reason is to reduce future competition by eliminating the possibility that the acquiring firm would have entered the acquired firm's market.

Example

A leading manufacturer of software, merges with an athletic shoes firm. The resulting company is faced with the same competition in each of its two markets after the merger as the individual firms were before the merger. One example of a conglomerate merger was the merger between the Walt Disney Company and the American Broadcasting Company.[7]

2.2. Acquisition

An Acquisition takes place when one company buys another company.

So, under an acquisition we understand the purchase of an enterprise or prats of an enterprise which occurs either through the transference of shares or through the transference all or certain economic goods and obligations of an enterprise or through the combination of both. Under it majority holdings as well as minority participation are summarized. With an Acquisition can be assumed from the fact that the economic independence is limited or is completely given up. The acquirer or bidder (so called a company which wants to merge or acquire with another one) either buys majority ownership of the shares of the target company or business operations and their assets.

---

[6] N.N, www.mbda.gov, 2015
[7] MBDA, www.mbda.gov, 2015

3. Deal Motivation

Money will always be an important and primary deal motivation of mergers and acquisitions. Besides money there are other motives like:

- **Operating Synergy**; Improve operating efficiency through economies of scale or scope by acquiring a customer, supplier, or competitor
- **Financial Synergy**; Lower cost of capital
- **Diversification**; Position the firm in higher-growth products or markets
- **Strategic Realignment**; Acquire capabilities to adapt more rapidly to environmental changes than could be achieved if they were developed internally
- **Hubris;** Acquirers believe their valuation of the target is more accurate than the market's, causing them to overpay by overestimating synergy
- **Buying undervalued assets;** Acquire assets more cheaply when the equity of existing companies is less than the cost of buying or building the assets
- **Managerialism;** Increase the size of a company to increase the power and pay of managers
- **Tax consideration**; Obtain unused net operating losses and tax credits and asset writeups, and substitute capital gains for ordinary income
- **Market power***; actions taken to boost selling prices above competitive levels by affecting either supply or demand*
- **Misvaluation***; investor overvaluation of acquirer's stock encourages M&As* [8]

3.1. Synergy

Synergy, or the potential financial benefit achieved through the combining of companies, is often a driving force behind a merger. Shareholders will benefit if a company's post-merger share price increases due to the synergistic effect of the deal. The expected synergy achieved through the merger can be attributed to various factors, such as increased revenues, combined talent and technology, or cost reduction.

The idea that when two companies fuse, the assets and value are higher than the sum of all in the separate companies. In the context of M&As (mergers and acquisitions) a synergy is the most generally used term. Synergy is "the value realized from the incremental cash flows

---

[8] Donald DePamphilis, Mergers, Acquisitions and other Restructuring Activities, p. 6
[9] DePamphilis, p.5

generated by combining two businesses."[9] There are two types of synergy, operating and financial synergy.

Operating synergy is made of economies of scope and economies of scale, which can be significant factors of shareholder wealth creation.

Economies of scale are cost savings by producing a higher rate of goods per unit. It is possible to distribute fixed costs by a higher output of one product. Fixed costs are, for example,

"depreciation of equipment and amortization of capitalized software, normal maintenance spending, and obligations such as interest expense, lease payments, long-term union, customer, and vendor contracts, and taxes"[9]. As a counter to fixed costs there are variable costs like raw materials, packaging, and many more.

Economies of scope are also cost savings. Those effects arise when the production of two or more goods or products is more favorable than producing the goods or products separately.

The company can share the inputs for example in financial and technological recourses or management and research and development. So it is cheaper to combine the product lines in one single enterprise than producing in different firms.[10]

"Financial synergy results from lower capital costs; this can be achieved three ways. First, by investing in unrelated businesses, which decreases the systematic risk of a company's investment portfolio; […], which postulates that [conglomerate] mergers reduce profit fluctuations and stabilize the income streams of the merged company; the risk of insolvency is therefore reduced. […]. Second, capital costs can be lowered by increasing a company's size, as larger companies usually have access to cheaper capital. Finally, lower capital costs may be realized by establishing an internal capital market in which a firm can exploit superior information and thus allocate capital more efficiently (Trautwein, 1990)."[11]

---

[9] DePamphilis, p.6
[10] DePamphilis, p.6
[11] Kathrin Bösecke, Value Creation in Mergers, Acquisitions, and Alliances, p. 39

3.2. Diversification

Table 1 - The Production Market- Matrix

Markets / Products	Current	New
Current	Lower growth/ Lower Risk	Higher Growth/Higher Risk (Related Diversification)
New	Higher Growth/Higher Risk (Related Diversification)	Highest Growth/Highest Risk (Unrelated Diversification)

If a company buys firms in other business markets or in different business categories, it calls diversification. Often a diversification is chosen in a merger and acquisition context because the firm want to have a bigger portfolio to offer more products. A diversification could create a financial synergy that can reduces the cost of capital, or it can allow a company to target completely new markets or outsource their product line. The product-market-matrix above shows you which main diversification options companies have.

A related Diversification for example is when your company is producing Hamburgers and you want to diversify into a company making French fries. It would be not that high risk or challenge on resources because Hamburgers and French fries are more or less similar. So the companies share manufacturing know-how, marketing and operational skills. Unrelated Diversification is a term which refers to the manufacture of diverse products which have no relation to each other.[12] An example of unrelated diversification in a business could be, for example, Tchibo, which is known as a coffee selling company but besides coffee it also offers clothes and kitchen equipment.

3.3. Strategic realignment

Firms use M&A's to make rapid adjustments to changes in their external environment such as regulatory changes and technological innovation. Political changes can be as well grounds for M&A. In creating new opportunities for growth or threatening to make legacy firms' primary lines of business regulatory changes and technological innovations have been major forces. Technological innovations create new products and industries. For example, tablet computers reduced the demand for desktop and notebook computers. Also the

---

[12] DePamphilis, p.8-9

smartphone encouraged the growth of handheld telecommunications devices while undercutting the point-and-shoot camera industry and threatening the popularity of alarm clocks, and MP3 players.

A classical reason for a consolidation exists in the possibility to win in market power. This could effect on both sides of the market activity: On buyers side a greater become enterprise rather able to move presuppliers to concessions with prices and conditions of delivery, than a smaller enterprise. On sellers side the enterprise could try to earn monopoly profits by raising the prices, or to expand its sales and as a result of also profit volume by the fact that it can shows complete ranges of articles in a market.[13]

3.4. Financial considerations

Whether merging, buying or a selling a business, the key consideration from a financial perspective is determining the value of your business. This is essential to ensure that you receive adequate compensation for your business.

They are many financial considerations for mergers and acquisitions. Aspects like the acquirer believes that the target is undervalued or booming stock markets. But also falling interest rates and tax benefits. The production of shares of the market by the purchase of rival business is as attractive. Instead of developing with difficulty new products or investing high sums in the development of a new market, the same result could be reached with reduced risk by an enterprise takeover.

3.5. Hubris

The hubris hypothesis forms the basis for all management motives. It assumes that the selfoverestimation of the single actors of the management leads to estimate the value of an enterprise better than the market and results with it inevitably in a value-destructive transaction. "For instance, something like 70 percent of all new businesses fail within three years."[14] Besides, the hypothesis begins in the purchase price, in particular of the takeover premium. Therefore, the operating management is consciously ready to pay more than other potential buyers. That readiness is based on two possible misjudgments: On the one hand structured enterprise lines are endangered to overrate synergy potentials, to the other hand

---

[13] Matthias Müller, Größenwahn oder rationale Strategie? - Motive für Fusionen
[14] Robert F. Bruner: Applied Mergers and Acquisitions, P. 75-76

they believe in own abilities which should be enable not to realize to available synergy potentials. Actually such a management does not act in the individual self-interest, but on account of the objectively predictable failure also not in the interest of the shareholders.

It is disproportionately to be assumed from the fact that only the management overestimates itself and pays a too high premium, because in such cases many other partners like the supervisory board, adviser and investment banks are defeated of the same misjudgment. Manager with routine in the M&A business particularly threatened to be defeated misjudgments. They simply transfer her experiences from already successfully carried out projects and could overrate.[15]

3.6. Tax Consideration

For offsetting the taxable income of firms that combine through M&A's tax benefits, for example loss carryforwards and investment tax benefits, can be used. Firms with accumulated losses may use acquires of firms to offset future profits generated by the combined firms. Unused tax credits can be used to lower future tax liabilities. "Additional tax savings are created due to the purchase method of accounting, which requires the book value of the acquired assets to be revalued to their current market value for purposes of recording the acquisition on the books of the acquire firm".[16]

As depreciation expense is deducted from revenue in calculating a firm's taxable income, these generally higher assets value will reduce the amount of future taxable income generated by the related companies. "However, the taxable nature of the transaction often plays a more important role in determining whether a merger takes place than do any tax benefits accruing to the acquirer. The seller may view the tax-free status of the transaction as a prerequisite for the deal to take place. A properly structured transaction can allow the target shareholders to defer any capital gain until the acquirer's stock received in exchange for their shares is sold."[17]

---

[15] Jansen, S. A. (2013): Mergers & Acquisitions: Eine strategische, organisatorische und kapitalmarkttheoretische Einführung, p. 58
[16] DePamphilis, p.12
[17] DePamphilis, p.10

4. Conclusion

We can summarize that there are a lot of motivations for mergers and acquisitions. Financial benefits are always the main motivations to merger or acquire. For example, there are tax considerations or because of operating synergy the operating efficiency would improve by economies of scale or scope. Because of financial synergy there would be a lower cost of capital. Positioning the firm in higher-growth markets to increase selling prices above competitive levels and if the size of the company will increase so the power and pay of managers will increase, too. Besides of the positive motivations there is also a negative motivation. A negative motivation calls hubris. This happens when acquirers believe that their estimated value of the target is more precise than the market's causing them to pay too much.

So mergers and acquisitions happens "due in part to their greater access to financing and their more liquid stock."[18]

---

[18] DePamphilis, p.11

Literature review

Bösecke, K. (2009): Value Creation in Mergers, Acquisitions, and Alliances, GABLER RESEARCH, 1st Edition

Bruner, R. F. (2004): Applied Mergers and Acquisitions, John Wiley & Sons, Inc

Coyle, B. (2000): Mergers & Acquisitions, Glenlake Publishing Company, Ltd, Fitzroy Dearborn Publishers

DePamphilis, D. M. (2012): Mergers, Acquisitions, and Other Restructuring Activities, 6th Edition, Elsevier Inc.

Jansen, S. A. (2013): Mergers & Acquisitions: Eine strategische, organisatorische und kapitalmarkttheoretische Einführung (5th ed.)

MBDA (n.d.): http://www.mbda.gov/blogger/mergers-and-acquisitions/5-types-companymergers, access data: 10/10/2015

Müller, M. (2000): http://www.boeckler.de/pdf/mbf_fusionsmanagement_groessenwahn.pdf, access data: 10/10/2015

Sherman, A. J. (2011): Mergers and Acquisitions from A to Z, 3rd Edition

WINTER MANAGEMENT CONSULTING GmbH (2009 - 2015): http://winter-mconsulting.at/de/kompetenzen/ma_post_merger_integration_pmi#top, access data: 10/12/2015